THE KAMA SUTRA FOR CATS

Translator's Note: This version of The Kama Sutra for Cats draws not only on the original 1869 "Nilajjata" translation by the great Indian adventurer and academic, Sir Vházzant Nérf, but also on the later commentary contained in the second edition of "Ah-smahlah Rhát." In keeping with both these works, the accents used in the transliterated Sanskrit text indicate where the vowel stress should be placed.

TEN SPEED PRESS
P.O. Box 7123, Berkeley, California 94707

Text © 1993 Burton Silver
Illustrations © 1993 Margaret Woodhouse

Library of Congress Catalog information is
on file with the publisher.

ISBN: 0-89815-553-3

Originated and devised by Burton Silver

Compiled by Silverculture Press
487 Karaka Bay Rd, Wellington 3
New Zealand

Book design - Trevor Plaisted
Editorial direction - Melissa da Souza-Correa
Translation assistance - Martin O'Connor

Printed and bound in Hong Kong.

1 2 3 4 5 - 97 96 95 94 93

THE KAMA SUTRA
FOR CATS

Burton Silver

Illustrations Margaret Woodhouse

Ten Speed Press

CONTENTS

KHATNIHVARNAH

The Land of Heavenly Humps

All cats know that to sleep in the warm softness of *Khatnihvárnah* is to experience absolute peace and ultimate refreshment. But the deep, life-giving heat pulsating from below into the feather-soft, deliciously yielding flocculence of the aromatic tundra above, is generated by awesome powers. Powers that continually shape and re-shape the land. Gigantic subterranean conglomerates shift restlessly beneath the surface, grinding together in a twisting, writhing, shuddering contest of forces that can create whole mountains in one spasm. So it is, that the cat must proceed with caution and know the 69 positions contained in *The Kama Sutra fah Puteekhátz.*

ZLUMBAH NUMBAHZ

The Sixty-nine Positions

The cat who ventures into the Land of Heavenly Humps without knowing the 69 *Zlumbáh Numbáhz* cannot achieve *Purvárnah*, the sleep of ultimate peace that provides the greatest health. For of all the lands, it is the most unpredictable and changeable and the cat must know and quickly adopt the many positions appropriate to its rapidly changing topographies if it is to retain its composure and remain unharmed.

But not only must the cat know the sixty-nine positions, it must also learn the many signs that tell of what to expect. It must know not to be fooled by the *dhub-dub*[1] which has the appearance of a tasty little washed-up fish, and it should be able to interpret sounds such as the quiet whispers of *sweet nhártinz* that warn of something about to come.

---

[1] Dhub-dub as in, "Rhábah dhub-dub, saree-men innah tubh."(Verse 46) The cat is clearly warned against tampering with the common rubbah or latex dhub-dub which it suggests are best dealt with by saree-men (literally men wearing dresses, probably Scottish Highlanders), who will deal with them in a jacuzzi.

But while the cat may be able to judge the nuance of the mighty purr, *znórin,* or perceive the subtle significance of the bark, *vhártin,* it will have no peace in *Khatnihvárnah* without knowledge of the *Ehtekhat.*

EHTEKHAT

A Code of Behavior

Unless a cat knows the code of behavior contained in the *Ehtekhat*, it shall not prosper in the Land of Heavenly Humps. "The cat who fails to conduct itself according to the rules, disturbs the equanimity of the land and incites the ire of the subterranean forces. Rapid expulsion from the land may result." (Verse 82)

The knowing cat will not approach the land directly but first sit apart from it in a state of repose and look upon it with disdain, lest it be thought wanton. It is at this time that the cat should conduct its toilet, for no cleaning, especially that involving strong rhythmical or noisy licking, will be tolerated in the land. Dribbling or sucking is considered slovenly, purring should be discreet at all times, and unseemly kneading[1] is not appropriate.

[1] Verse 85 mentions two types of kneading. When the cat kneads on Bhigabitz "The Soft Mountains of Joy" that border Kleevidj, it is called, "The Baker Kneading the Dough." Provided claws are withdrawn many Bakers are tolerated and at times actively encouraged. However when the kneading is performed in Dah-krutj, "The Dark Place of Tender Fruit," it is known as, "The Vintner Pressing Grapes." This is never tolerated as it may lead to Khlord-borlz, one of the nine life-threatening disharmonies.

No food may be brought onto the land, especially recently killed prey, or parts of prey, no matter how well displayed. There shall be no hissing, fighting, meowing or scratching of any kind. (Vigorous under-chin scratching is particularly tactless as it vibrates the land and may confuse the underground forces.) The *Ehtekhat* regards claw sharpening as barbaric, playing and pouncing as vulgar, and vigorous tail movements as coarse. (Allowing the tip of the tail to enter *Ghob*, the small pink cave with white bars, is of the utmost discourtesy.) Finally, it is in extremely poor taste for any cat to enter the land while moulting.

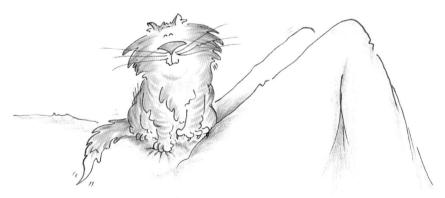

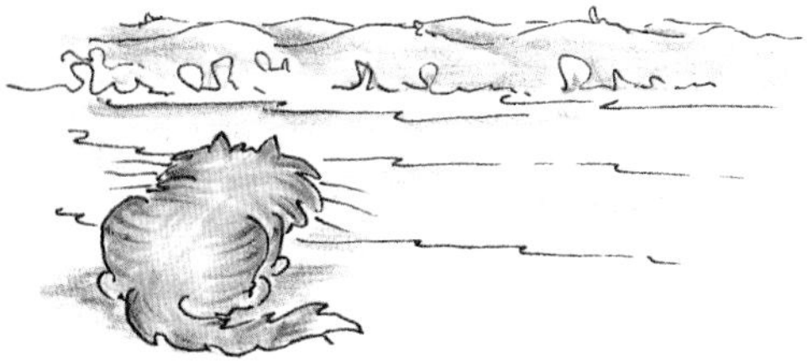

PART ONE

A JOURNEY IN HUDVHARTA

The Sea of Warm Waves

When the humps begin to undulate rhythmically, at first like the gentle giggling of ripples dancing and sparkling in the sun, and then, later, like the heavy moody waves heaving and tossing in the mighty ocean; and when a deep moaning wind accompanies their final crashing, hot and foaming on the shore; then it is called *Hudvhárta* or *The Sea of Warm Waves.*

Verse 216. The Kama Sutra fah Puteekhátz.

HARTANSVETTEE

The Hot and Stormy Sea

When the mighty wind, the howling, screaming, moaning, snorting wind, whips up the waves into a thrashing, slapping, hot frenzy, it is called *Hártansvettee* or *The Hot and Stormy Sea*. In this turgid state, the sea provides the greatest amount of health-giving warmth, though not without obvious dangers. Cats must read the waves carefully before attempting to enjoy its steamy delights.

ABUL BODID ZEHMIN

Position Twenty-one

When the knowing cat carefully searches the thrashing waves of *Hártansvettee* for a suitably flexible boat in which to ride the wild seas, and then guides her crew aboard, it is called *Abul Bodid Zéhmin*. While their ride may be rough it is nevertheless deliciously hot and rhythmically soothing while it lasts.[1]

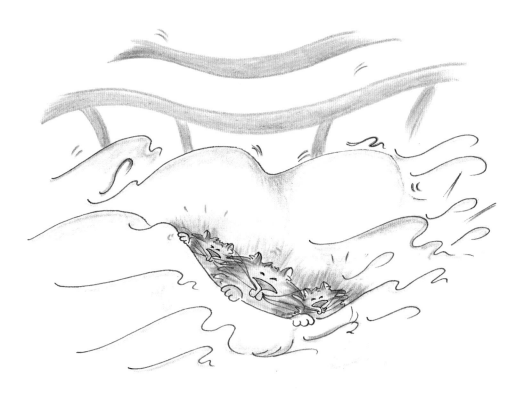

[1] Warning that the storm is about to abate prematurely is often heralded by a wind sound like, "Ayem Védhee Sáree, butaiv Khum Ulreydeh!" The likelihood of another storm building up in these circumstances is remote. This is known as "Da Khum befardah Stum," which we are told is very common.

SAILAH VEE

Position Twenty-two

When cats of little knowing jump into the stormy sea without first checking if a suitable ship is sailing, it is called *Sailah Vee* or *The Lubbers' Leap*. Cats who dare to board ships[1] without reserving berths are quickly tossed off.

[1] Shipez, as in "Dah liddel Bopeepez Av-lust dare shipez." The Kama Sutra fah Puteekhátz warns that vicarious lust is incompatible with daring or rashly made bookings on unsuitable ships and will inevitably result in small Peeping Toms losing their little boats or shipez.

VASHYAFAHNI

The Sandy Shore

When the waves are pressed closely alongside each other and then drawn to one side so as to leave a large flat area, it is known as *Vashyafáhni* or *The Sandy Shore*. When the tide is out the shore provides ample room for the more extravagant positions of repose. But dangers are also present and cats must take due consideration of the *Tahm-an-taidh*[1] or the sudden surges so common in *Vashyafáhni*.

[1] Verse 287 of the Kama Sutra fah Puteekhátz clearly warns of dangers such as Vayt-fah or total purging resulting from a lack of understanding of Tahm-an-taidh. The phrase, "Tahm-an-taidh vayt-fah kno-khat," rather too lyrically translated by Fheel Whood, 1920, Oxford version, as "sudden surges urge purges," hardly goes far enough in seriously warning the cat that purging may be so powerful as to bring about its complete disappearance or Kno-khat.

SAHIB SURPHER

Position Twenty-six

When the knowing cat who wishes to gain the blissful heat of the warm waves of *Vashyafáhni* lies with its chest on the shore and its haunches against the waves, it is called *Sahib Surpher.* The waves pass harmlessly beneath *Sahib Surpher* and their rolling action soothes his underbelly. Sleep is undisturbed.[1]

[1] Verse 296 specifies certain sounds borne on the wind which may just precede a slowly encroaching wave and thereby act as a warning to the cat. Sounds include: "Aw Khárm-on!" Followed by, "Nooh! Aye-ghotta edaik!" Or "Eetz yawtirn tu-lyin di vetzpoht!" Followed by "Lai-khal-itiz!"

23

SIDDIN DHAK

Position Twenty-seven

When the cat of little knowing lies with his back pressed close against the warm waves and with his head twisted as if looking up something, in the manner typical of an *Idiat Skert Vatcha* or pervert of little brain, it is called *The Siddin Dhák*.
When the waves crash over him he is squashed and rolled up like a sausage.[1]

[1] Warning of the dire consequences of being so squashed is clearly given, as the sausage in this case is the Dhep-bluzée, a long, thin, hard sausage much loved by the Bedouin courtiers of Devahl, as in, "Kort Bedouin da Devahl ana Dhep-bluzée."

PART TWO

A JOURNEY IN BIRNYAFAHNI

The Desert of Burning Sand

Wh
hen the humps lie low and rounded like slowly shifting dunes, hissing
softly to one another with their falling
sands; and when all the air is still and
filled with the languid sighs of spent
ruins and lost dreams; when hot winds
suddenly tear the sands apart, hot, biting winds that send camels hurrying
awkwardly through the night and set
the Bedouins' tents to noisy flapping;
then it is called *Birnyafáhni* or *The Desert
of Hot Sand.*

Verse 271. The Kama Sutra fah Puteekhátz.

NHEE TREMBLAH

The Camel that Sways

When two tall humps of equal size rise up in the middle of the land and begin to move slowly from side to side in the ungainly manner of an upright inebriate, it is called *Nhée Tremblah* or *The Camel that Sways and Trembles in the Hot Sand.* It is best to ride the camel when it is standing still, which it does when chewing its cud. The cat will quickly recognize this phase from the rather obvious eating noises and little moans of satisfaction it makes. *Nhée Tremblah* should never be ridden between its humps.[1]

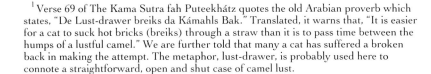

[1] Verse 69 of The Kama Sutra fah Puteekhátz quotes the old Arabian proverb which states, "De Lust-drawer breiks da Kámahls Bak." Translated, it warns that, "It is easier for a cat to suck hot bricks (breiks) through a straw than it is to pass time between the humps of a lustful camel." We are further told that many a cat has suffered a broken back in making the attempt. The metaphor, lust-drawer, is probably used here to connote a straightforward, open and shut case of camel lust.

LAH-WRENS OFAH RAPIER

Position Thirty-three

When the knowing cat crouches on the top of one hump it is known as *Lah-wrens ofah Rápier*,[1] or *The Arabian Knight*. When the humps come together, and come they will when the camel delights in the ecstasy of some tasty fig leaves, the cat is safe, and several cats may even rub soothingly against one another.

 [1] Lah-wrens ofah Rápier, literally, "birds of a sword." Unlike birds of a feather who flock together, birds of a sword, stay aboard. A clear reference to being able to maintain balance while travelling on these "Ships of the desert."

HUMPATEE DHUMPATEE

Position Thirty-four

When the cat of little knowing hopes to enjoy the trance-like tingles of *Nhée Tremblah*, and drapes itself over the hump in a languid manner, it is called *Humpatée Dhumpatée*[1] or *Old Egg Face*. When the humps come together, and come they will, the cat will be caught in between and cracked like an egg.

 [1] This great anti-hero from the well-known fertility legend is often involved in couplings that are decidedly kinky, such as with older horses and older men. As in, "Oldah Kinkz Oziz an Oldah Kinkz Mehn." (Verse 291)

BEDOUIN DASHEETZ

The Bedouin Tent

When a large and flimsy mound rises up in the land and begins to sway and flap in the hot desert wind; when the muffled cries and grunts of Bedouins gaily feasting and drinking can be heard; and when Goozi,[1] the tiny pink mouse, who guards the jewels, can be seen darting here and there to snatch up the delicious crumbs of spicy crumpet; then it is called *Bedouin Dashéetz* or *The Bedouin Tent*.

[1] Verse 78 refers to the great freedom accorded Goozi the mouse: "Goozi, Goozi, Ghanda, Vidah shálya vonda, Upzterz an dhanzterz, Inmah lud-eeze chumbar." Here the mouse, son of Ghanda is called and bidden to run up and down in the tastefully appointed chumbar, a type of low-lit cavernous watering hole for male friends, such as Weevily Vinkhee. (Lud-eeze; literally a lot of ease, refers to a chumbar that provides a great deal of relaxation). Strict rules prevent the mouse taking the jewels, which it guards, into the lud-eeze chumbar. Any attempt by the cat to get at the mouse while it is in there would be interpreted by the Bedouins as an attempt to get at the unprotected jewels and be vigorously repulsed.

PEETAH PATTAH

Position Thirty-seven

When the knowing cat taps the tent lightly like the pitter patter of falling rain so as to wake[1] Goozi the little pink mouse, it is known as *Peetah Pattah*. The cat who indulges in sensitive paw play will be rewarded with a growing friendship.

[1] The 1869 Chinese translation (edited by Eric Shin), refers to a special double-curry recipe for sausages (dhorks), which is claimed to be very effective in getting Goozi up on time. "He-curry, De-curry Dhork" evidently strikes the number one chord with pink mice who cannot resist hot dishes, and is fabled to get them going up and down immediately.

BHIG OFFENDI

Position Thirty-eight

When the cat of little
knowing pounces on Goozi
the mouse instead of
skilfully enticing[1] him
out for a friendly game,
it is called the
Bhig Offendi.
Being unaware
that Goozi guards the
Bedouins' jewels and
always sleeps on top of
them, he is in for a rude
shock, as is Goozi.

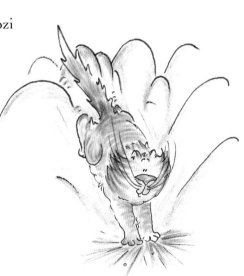

 [1] Verse 47 includes the well known adage, "Doily bhard khatchez dah verm," which clearly refers to the fact that sycophantic opera singers are sometimes useful for enticing vermin such as mice, though being early, as opposed to premature, obviously helps.

39

PART THREE

A JOURNEY IN CHILYAFAHNI

The Mountains of Feathery Snow

Whater all the land is heaved up into great rounded mountains and covered with sheets of ice that shimmer in the pale light; and when musk-scented vapors drift from the glowing hot fissures and fumeroles in the caves beneath and gather in moist clouds that hang mysteriously above the deep moaning valleys; then it is called *Chilyafáhni* or *The Mountains of Feathery Snow.*

Verse 345. The Kama Sutra fah Puteekhátz.

KHOLD KUMFATAH

The Snowy Mountain of Joy

When all the land is heaped up into a great mountain of lumpy snow, so deep and so soft it feels as if it were made of millions of little downy feathers, then it is called *Khold Kúmfatah* or *The Snowy Mountain of Joy*. Great care must be exercised in ascending[1] to the warm crater on its summit.

[1] Verse 76 refers to the "Klarm-akz arf dah bigh ársendh." The term Klarm-akz has been variously interpreted to mean either, a climbing-axe needed for the big ascent, or, the joy experienced by the cat after making the big ascent. Neither is correct. The Klarm-akz is rather something experienced by, or integral to, The Mountain of Joy itself, and the cat should be wary of it.

43

DAH MEOW-TINEERS

Position Forty-eight

When the knowing cats climb carefully, one at a time, up the ridges[1] without using their claws it is called *The Meow-tineers* or the way of *Saredmun Dhilary*. On reaching the summit[2] they may enjoy the sleep of great stillness and awake refreshed.

[1] Verse 345 warns cats to beware of Awk kazzimz, a clear reference to the numerous chasms that form between the ridges and act as home to some rather noisy hawks. While these hawks are seldom seen they can emit a great variety of sounds, from piercing screams to deep truncated squawks, which can be very disconcerting to the unwary feline climber.

[2] The mountaineering cat may sometimes catch sight of the exquisite little alpine buds, better known as the fabled Idle Mice, who are found sitting pretty on the twin peaks that border the valley of Kleevidj (see page 10). Under no circumstances should these be plucked for they are not what they seem.

DJAK ARNJIL

Position Forty-nine

W hen the cats of little knowing all scramble up the
mountain together and hang on with their claws it is known
as *Djak Arnjil*[1]. This often results in the entire covering of
snow being pulled off in a giant all-engulfing
avalanche which may reveal the
subterranean forces. They will
be greatly angered,
especially if the cats'
claws have torn
at the snow and
released clouds
of fluffy
feather-like
snowflakes.

[1] Djak Arnjil, the small-brained feline hermaphrodite who, according to legend foolishly climbs up to fetch water when common sense dictates climbing down to find it. Djak Arnjil eventually falls down, and while he sustains some head damage, we are assured that his seemingly futile up and down activity is not without a degree of pleasurable release. Indeed the fallen cat is greeted, somewhat prematurely perhaps, with the phrase, "Eee Djak yhule-ate!" An obvious instruction to let go of his load (water-pail?) and come and enjoy the feast of The Giant Festive Log.

47

SNUGGLAHS' KHAVZ

The Caves of Warm Desire

When voluptuous voids are formed between the valley folds at the foot of The Mountain of Feathery Snow; and when these voids have enticing openings that turn into wilfully winding passages of great warmth and constantly changing direction; and when they lead to deliciously hot caverns inhabited by The Strange Hairy Ones or Snugglahs[1] who keep fighting and trying to push each other out of the way, it is called, *Snugglahs' Khavz* or *The Caves of Warm Desire*.

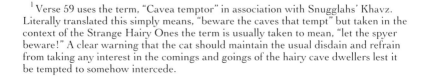

[1] Verse 59 uses the term, "Cavea temptor" in association with Snugglahs' Khavz. Literally translated this simply means, "beware the caves that tempt" but taken in the context of the Strange Hairy Ones the term is usually taken to mean, "let the spyer beware!" A clear warning that the cat should maintain the usual disdain and refrain from taking any interest in the comings and goings of the hairy cave dwellers lest it be tempted to somehow intercede.

49

UNDAH-KARVAH KOP

Position Fifty-three

When the knowing cat who wishes to enjoy the deep heat of Snugglahs' Khavz first enters backwards with great care and ensures that his face protrudes at all times, it is called *The Undah-Kharvah Kop*. From this position he can exit quickly and safely[1] should a cave-in occur.

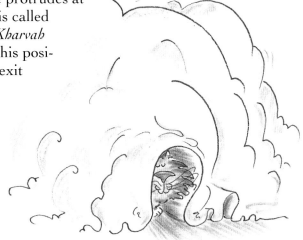

[1] Verse 68 includes the phrase "Azfhat aza pinkh-ache," which warns the cat to beware of any very pink areas in the cave which may become fat and aching. Under these circumstances there is a heightened risk of being squashed flat.

51

KHATAZ TROFEE

Position Fifty-four

When the cat of little knowing rushes head-first into the cave and pushes herself eagerly along the warm passages until she finds a hot place of rest, it is known as *The Khatáz Trofee*. Made drowsy by the heat, and with no obvious exit, she may be severely pummelled[1], especially if the Hairy Ones begin fighting.

[1] Verse 72 contains the lines, "Zinga-zonga sikh pantz, Ah-por-khat fulla rhy."
Zinga-zonga describes the rapid (zinging) back and forth motion the cat will
experience and compares it to being trapped inside the tight pants of an energetic
sikh. This results in the cat feeling as if it's been stuffed with a loaf of rye bread.

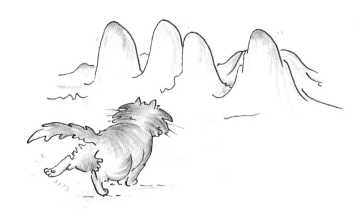

PART FOUR

A JOURNEY IN BHUMPYAFAHNI

The Deep Canyons of Delight

When all the land is lifted up into soaring hot columns that shimmer in the midday sun; and when their sheer walls suddenly reverberate to the rhythmic thunder of wild horses galloping along the warm meandering pathways below; then it is called *Bhúmpyafáhni* or *The Deep Canyons of Delight*.

Verse 645. The Kama Sutra fah Puteekhátz.

DAH KRUTJ

The Dark Groove of Glee

When the narrow pathway at the foot of the canyon begins to heave and shake as if great boulders were being hurled along it; and when the canyon walls appear to lurch about as if the very earth were moving, then it is called *Dah Krutj*[1], or *The Dark Groove of Glee*.

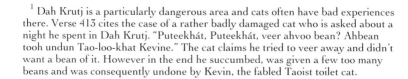

[1] Dah Krutj is a particularly dangerous area and cats often have bad experiences there. Verse 413 cites the case of a rather badly damaged cat who is asked about a night he spent in Dah Krutj. "Puteekhát, Puteekhát, veer ahvoo bean? Ahbean tooh undun Tao-loo-khat Kevine." The cat claims he tried to veer away and didn't want a bean of it. However in the end he succumbed, was given a few too many beans and was consequently undone by Kevin, the fabled Taoist toilet cat.

KLOORZ ANAFEKT

Position Fifty-seven

When the knowing cat nestles in the warm groove at the bottom of the canyon with her four paws resting on its sides, it is known as *Kloorz Anafékt*. Should the walls of the canyon press in on her, the cat is able to ensure they quickly retreat by simply extending her claws.[1]

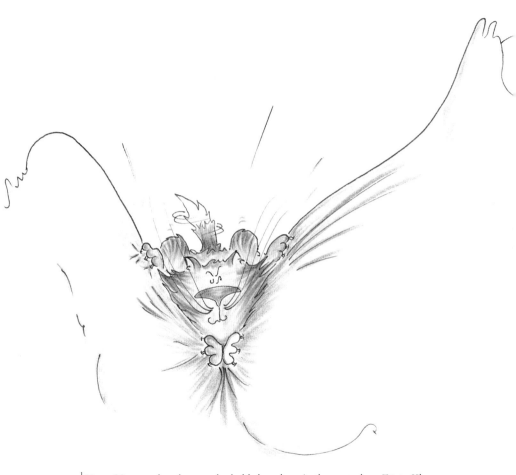

 [1] Verse 98 notes that the cat who holds her claws in the central, or Zénta Kloorz position, ensures that she will not be crushed and mushed up should the canyon walls suddenly rush together. This is known as avoiding the Krush Mush Raj. 59

Dah Loinz Shearh

Position Fifty-eight

When the cat of little knowing stretches herself out expansively like a big cat who owns it all, it is called taking *Dah Loinz Shearh*.[1]

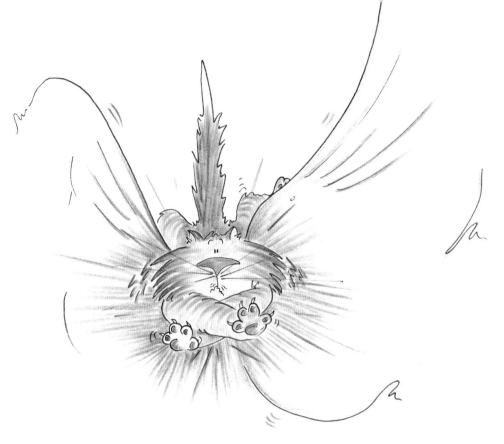

[1] Taking Dah Loinz Shearh is usually interpreted as taking the chance of being caught and shorn in half by the scissor action of dah loinz. Just what sort of loinz are referred to here is not exactly clear. While the position is undoubtedly similar to being caught between Enhemee Loinz, it is not quite the same as being caught Hookh-loin und Zinker, though this does seem to be a Foin-loin.

61

BHARKIN BONKO

The Rodeo Dog

When all the land echoes with the crashing of hooves and the snorting of fiery nostrils; and when the ground shudders as the wild stallion surges forward into the corral; and when his head lashes at the earth in a wild screaming frenzy that threatens to warn the whole world of his coming; then it is called *Bhárkin Bonko* or *The Rodeo Dog.*[1]

[1] The three major hazards likely to be encountered by the cat are summed up in Verse 93. "Eezbhuk, eezverze dah-kneez bhyte." It is difficult to ascertain which is the most devastating of the three: the horse's buck, his poetry, or his biting knees.

RHUMPEE PUMPEE

Position Sixty-three

When the knowing cat, approaches the bucking horse from behind[1] and jumps lightly from the fence onto its back before holding on gently with its front paws, it is known as *Rhumpee Pumpee.*

[1] Verse 87 contains the line, "Dun puteekhát befuddah órz." A warning to the cat not to get right in front of a bucking steed. This will inevitably befuddle (befuddah) the horse and lead to the cat getting done-in in the process.

VHANKEE DILDO

Position Sixty-four

When the cat of little knowing rests its head on the warm expansive rump of the horse and does not use the reins[1] during the gallop, it is known as *Vhankee Dildo*. Some cats suffer lifelong disorientation from the severe vibrations imparted when riding in this position.

[1] The inevitable result of this practice is outlined in Verse 187. "Rhein-goh, rhein-goh órzes, ahh phoor Khat-fullah pózzez." Clearly if it lets the horse's reins go, the poor cat will end up adopting a great number of poses in very quick succession. The verse goes on to suggest the use of a tissue if the cat should fall down.

PART FIVE

A SHORT JOURNEY IN KHUDDILYAFAHNI

The Land of Fluffy Clouds

When a great silence descends upon the land; when all is calm and all is still; and when little billowy white clouds hover just above the plains, their fluffy-soft edges gleaming in the silver moonlight; then it is called *Khuddilyafáhni* or *The Land of Fluffy Clouds*.

Verse 673. The Kama Sutra fah Puteekhátz.

DAH ZILVAH LOININ

The Edge of Bliss

Clouds do not last long and the cat must decide quickly how to use them before they vanish. Truly it is said, "Better to be laid on the fluffy clouds and take your pleasure now, than wait, and hope for bliss in Heaven." Or in the simple words of *The Kama Sutra fah Puteekhátz,* "Bhetta laed dun Nirvana."

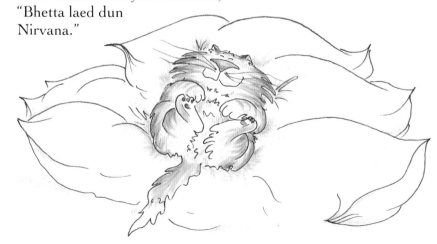

However, the cat that cuddles the cloud
into an image of itself in order to experience
The Eternal Snuggle of Bliss[1], must learn to let go
lest it be cast adrift and lost forever.

---

[1] Verse 99 contains the lines, "Twoinkle, Twoinkle, leekhil Tzar, Meow Ivan dah fartcha ah." This ancient Sanskrit rhyme tells the story of the Russian Pig-king who oinks blissfully after a huge meal of leeks. Ivan the cat meows in wonder as he watches him float aloft on the fluffy featherbed of his own flatulence. (The only way that pigs might fly).